If I Had Wings

Inspired Writings
By
Sandra J Yearman

SERAPHIM PUBLISHING LLC

WE WILL BRING LIGHT TO ALL THE DARK PLACES

Registered trademark-
Sandra J Yearman
Seraphim Publishing
438 Water St. Cambridge, WI 53523

Copyright © 2008 Sandra J Yearman
Produced in the United States of America
Author : Sandra J Yearman
Editor: Sandra J Yearman
Cover Design by Sandra J Yearman
Layout and design by Sandra J Yearman

All rights reserved. No part of this book may be reproduced, stored in or introduced into a retrieval system, or transmitted, in any form or by any means, electronic or mechanical, including photocopying or recording or otherwise copied for public or private use—other than for "fair use" as brief quotations embodied in articles and reviews--without written permission from the author.

Library of Congress Control Number: 2009906922
ISBN: 978-0-9815791-9-1
First Edition

To The Holiest Of Hosts
The Answer To All
May Your Holy Presence
Fill These Pages
And Touch All Who Read Them
Amen
Amen
Amen

CONTENTS

DEDICATION

If I Had Wings..7
Bless Those Who Thirst...........................11
The Living Flames Of Heaven 13
Angels And Old Lace................................16
Bless This Family.......................................19
I Will..20
God's Winged Messengers.......................22
Sanctuaries Of Holiness...........................24

SEEKING LIGHT IN THE DARKNESS

Jesus Would I Have Stood Before You....28
The Masses...31
Without Names...33
In The Flames..35
Our Children...38
World Filled With Grace..........................40
War Changes..42
God Stand Before.....................................45
God You Never Left Us...........................48

CONTENTS

Torn Between Worlds 50
Temptation..52
The Demons Smile..................................54
Carry Us Through All Our Years............58
Screams In Silence..................................62
Destruction...64

COMING HOME

Lord Thank You 69
Love Without Boundaries.......................70
Shatter The Death Masks.......................72
Bless Me With Your Majesty..................73
With My Voice...75
I Seek Your Face.....................................77
The Holy Promise Of God.....................79
Lord I Come Before You........................81
Help Me Never To Forget.......................82
Open Our Hearts To Your Gifts.............84
Angels Protect 85

Dedication

If I Had Wings Lord

If I had wings Lord
If I had wings
If I had wings Lord
If I had wings

I'd chase the devil back into the pit
I'd chase that devil back into the hole
I'd take my wings and cover it
And we wouldn't see that devil no more, no more

If I had wings Lord
If I had wings
If I had wings Lord
If I had wings

I would spread them out, Lord
To cover Your children everywhere
To give them shelter from the storm
To pray You keep them in Your care

If I had wings Lord
If I had wings
If I had wings Lord
If I had wings

I would carry Your creations
There would be room for them all
I would carry them to You
To answer Your Call

If I had wings Lord
If I had wings
If I had wings Lord
If I had wings

I would pray for all creation
Until the end of days
To keep all men and all nations
In Your Holy Ways

If I had wings Lord
If I had wings
If I had wings Lord
If I had wings

I would sing, Lord
I would sing Your Song
And I would teach Your children
To correct what is wrong

If I had wings Lord
If I had wings
If I had wings Lord
If I had wings

I would dance, Lord
To the Song from above
To the music of Heaven
The Song filled with Love

Amen Amen Amen

Bless Those Who Thirst

God please give shelter to
Those without shelter this night

Please provide homes for
Those who are homeless

Please send Your nourishment to
Those who hunger

Please Bless
Those who thirst for You

God bring Your children Home

And I will give Your creation shelter

And I will provide them with a home

And I will feed them

And I will help to bring Your children Home, my Father

Amen Amen Amen

The Living Flames Of Heaven

The lights that brighten this world
Are often Heaven sent
To guide us through our darkness
As only God has meant

These lights are blessings
That are sent from above
Regardless of their forms
They are sent with God's true Love

A Love that has no boundaries
A Love that can not be contained
In the frailties of these worlds
To save us from our pain

The living flames of Heaven
Can take on any guise
Open up your hearts
And God's signs you will recognize

See the uniqueness of creation
See the hearts behind the masks
See the Holiness of life
To care is not a task

God can speak in whispers
God can speak in roars
Holiness abounds us
Love and Mercy soars

Hold the hand that is offered
Wipe away the tears
Love the ones discarded
Dissolve the darkest fears

The lights that brighten this world
Are often Heaven sent
To guide us through the darkness
As only God has meant

Amen Amen Amen

Angels And Old Lace

Christmas is a time of Grace
Of Love and Mercy unbound
A time for us to remember
The Home that we have found

Each culture has its symbols
Of this most Holy holiday
When God blessed all creation
And showed us the Holy Way

There are symbols that represent giving
There are symbols that represent life
A time of reflection and hope
That we can escape this strife

My trees have become rituals
They represent God's Grace
As I wrap them in gold and pearls
With Angels and old lace

The top represents Holiness
Surrounded by Mercy and Grace
Covered with Forgiveness
Angels and old lace

The lights represent the Spirit
Lighting our dark ways
The branches are filled with Love
That God shows us all our days

Ringed with Holy Compassion
Filled with delight
The tree is brilliance
That lights the darkest night

Although our symbols vary
As long as they represent the gifts sent from above
To help us remember
God's Blessings and His Love

Amen Amen Amen

Bless This Family

Bless this Holy family
Fill us with Your Grace
Save us from the darkness
Help us seek Your Face

Let this home be filled with Angels
To guard us through the night
To touch all who enter here
To protect us with God's Might

Carry us wherever we may go
Bless us with Love and Peace
Watch our children as they grow
From darkness we release

Amen Amen Amen

I Will

Jesus there will always be a place for
You at my table
There will always be a room for You in
my home
There will always be a place for You in
my heart
There will always be...

Jesus I will follow Your teachings
I will follow Your Word
I will follow Your Way
I will follow...

Jesus I will sing Your praise
I will sing Your Honor
I will sing Your Song
I will sing...

I will believe...

Amen Amen Amen

God's Winged Messengers

God's winged messengers
Will bring His children Home
Creation will rejoice
The worlds will align
Heaven will sing praises

When we have passed the tests
When we have fulfilled our purpose
When we have been transformed
God's winged messengers will bring
His children Home

When we have removed the dark
obstacles
Which prevent us from seeking
God's Face

When we have overcome this world
By Faith, Forgiveness and Love

We will hear the Voice of God
Sending His winged messengers
To bring us Home

Amen Amen Amen

Sanctuaries Of Holiness

Sanctuaries of Holiness
Tabernacles of Faith
Songs of the Heavens
Divinity and Grace

Faith carries always
Towards Heaven and King
Chants of the Holy men
Through ages do ring

Flames of the Spirit
Fire of God
Lord of the hosts
The staff and the rod

Shepherd and King
Majesty behold
Father, Redeemer
Savior fore told

Mysteries and mystics
Legacies of Kings
Words of the prophets
Angels do sing

The tree of the living
The scrolls of the dead
The answer of ancients
The words that God said

The Alpha, Omega
The Poet and King
The Dawn and the Star
And the Truth that they bring

The question, the answer
One In Threefold
The Word and the Song
And the promises as told

Amen Amen Amen

Seeking Light In The Darkness

Jesus Would I Have Stood Before You

Jesus I read
That no one defended You
That no one stood before You
That You were betrayed, defiled and denied

And I wonder Lord, what I would have done
Would my fears have been so great
that I would stand motionless and
watch You taken away

Would my fears have been so
overwhelming that I would have
denied You

Would my faith have been so weak
That I would not have cried out
That I would not have tried to stop the torture

That I would not have asked to take
Your place

Jesus I am filled
With guilt
With shame

How could they not have known
How could they have stood by as You were defiled
How could they not have acted

How can we stand by now

Lord God help us to overcome our
guilt and fear
Help us to overcome our horror and
pain
Help us to heal

Lord God
Forgive us and Bless us

Amen Amen Amen

The Masses

Hear the cry of the masses
Lost and alone
Stumbling in the chaos
Looking for a home

Listen as they hunger
Watch as they cry
Wandering in these worlds
In pain and afraid to die

Light is all around them
Yet they fail to see
That God is always with us
And can set us free

Is it that they are afraid to ask Him
Or call upon His Name
Do they only believe what is before
their eyes
Are they too filled with shame

What does it take for them to
understand
What does it take for them to believe
There is more to this world
Than what their eyes perceive

Amen Amen Amen

Without Names

Let us pray for the
Forsaken and the forgotten
For those without names

For the lost and abused
For the dead and dying
For the littered bodies in these dark
worlds

Let us pray that God
Will send us stars, as beacons
To bring us Light in these dark times
To illuminate our pathways Home

Let us pray
That we will hear God's Voice always
That we will follow His Path, His Way
That the Holy Spirit will ignite
within us

The Spirit
The passion
The Fire of the Lord

That all of Heaven will illuminate
these dark worlds

Amen Amen Amen

In The Flames

'God help me find my way out'
The fire fighter prayed
As he stumbled through the darkness
As the fiery ashes sprayed

He was scorched by the heat
The flames billowed out of control
He prayed to God to save him
To keep his eternal soul

The Angel touched him gently
He thought that he was dead
'Am I going to Heaven'
Are the words he said

She kissed him on forehead
He felt his life return
'Take my hand and follow'
'You will not be burned'

He could barely see in the darkness
But he felt her presence near
She led him through the building
He heard his comrades cheer

'We thought that we had lost you'
'We could not find a way'
'The destruction was total'
Are the words he heard them say

He looked but could not find her
The messenger who had led
Him through the burning inferno
But he remembered the words she said

'God is always with you'
'Pray and He will hear'
'Believe in His Love'
'And He will keep you near'

Amen Amen Amen

Our Children

God save our children
Protect them from our sins
Cleanse them with Your Holiness
Remind them from where they begin

Let them not suffer
From the sins of their fathers
Help them to change these worlds
Help them to progress farther

Help them to conquer the darkness
Help them to see through the night
Remind them of their holiness
Help them to seek the Light

Let them be carried by Angels
Let them sing Your Holy Song
Let them desire the Light
Help them to change what is wrong

God save our children

Amen Amen Amen

World Filled With Grace

So afraid of the future
They lose sight of today
Crippled by their fears
Lost along the way

Searching for what they know not
Afraid to seek the Truth
No mystics or monks among them
Life is but a ruse

Delusions to deal with the pain
Distractions from life
Fear dictates all that is done
Life consists of strife

Heavenly Father help us
To conquer these dark tests
Give us the strength of warriors
Help us to do our best

Give us the hearts of Angels
And all this darkness would be replaced
With a world filled with Love
With a world filled with Grace

Amen Amen Amen

War Changes

They return from the wars
Changed within and without
Their families need healing
Their nightmares cry out

When the atrocities are committed
When the decisions are made
The consequences unequaled
The prices are paid

The families of warriors
Suffer in pain
For one that is lost
Is anything gained

The warriors, the heroes
Who die in the streets
Their comrades, their brethren
Forever to meet

God Bless the
Warriors who stand for us all
In the wars and the conflicts
Both great and both small

God heal the families
Who give without end
Who sacrifice
Their women and men

God Bless our nation
Let us be strong
A light in the darkness
May we all sing Your Song

Amen Amen Amen

God Stand Before

God I pray to You to stand before all
the Holy altars
In all the worlds that ever were
In all the worlds that ever will be
In all times, in all ages and in all
creation

God I pray to You to protect Your
Holy families
No matter their color
No matter their language
No matter which of Your Holy Names
they call upon You

God protect them from tyranny
Protect them from hatred, fear and ignorance
Protect them from the demons in this world

Darkness should never dictate who can worship
Fear should never prevent a child from praying to You
Ignorance, apathy and fear should not excuse others to stand-by while such atrocities occur in this world

God how do we empower darkness,
when we cower in fear and allow it to
prevent us from Holy worship
God let the power of Heaven prevail in
these dark worlds
God send the Holy Spirit to ignite
within all Your creation

God let the seeds of faith be planted
and flourish until life prevails over
death
Forgive us for the darkness we bring
upon ourselves and others

God save us

Amen Amen Amen

God You Never Left Us

God You never left us
Though many think that is true

God You never left us
It is us, who left You

We put up so many obstacles
That we can no longer see Your Face

We put up so many obstacles
Man's fall from Holy Grace

Our voices cry from the darkness
Our bodies are filled with pain

God empty out these prisons
God break our darkest chains

Help us to break through these obstacles
Help us to tear the high places down

Bless us with Your Holiness
Save us with Your Crown

Amen Amen Amen

Torn Between Worlds

They return from the horror
Not as they left
Disfigured and wounded
Torn and adrift

Chaos and casualties
Tears and the cries
At war and at home
As the human spirit tries

To conquer the darkness
To set this world free
The blood and the sweat
God we need help from Thee

What is it that we value
What gives us safe release
God carry us in battle
Strengthen our beliefs

There are wars in many countries
There are wars in many homes
There are wars in many spirits
God we need Your Loving Mercy to Atone

God bless us and cleanse us
Heal our disgrace
Torn between worlds
We need Your guiding Grace

Amen Amen Amen

Temptation

The face of the demon is always at hand
He deceives us with power, privilege and might
He deceives us with false illusions
When there is chaos and lies in the night

He offers that which he has no power to offer
He lures us with his treachery
He controls us with our fears
He seduces with his lechery

He wears many faces
The masks of the dead
He walks in many worlds
Of which it was said

That darkness will stalk us
But we can be saved by God's Grace
Lord heal and forgive us
Save us from this dark place

Amen Amen Amen

The Demons Smile

He rapes his children
And murders his wife
He says he is innocent
Because he had a hard life

My God is bigger
And better they say
Then they murder our children
While they are at play

And the demons smile

Bomb the innocent
Shoot the weak
Poison the children
Crucify the meek

Burn this village
Their color is wrong
We will show the world
Which color is strong

And the demons smile

The politicians say they will help
And steer us right
But they bring ignorance and chaos
Into the night

War after war
Yet little is freed
We are all victims
Of hatred and greed

And the demons smile

Masquerading demons
Claiming to be the holy way
Seducing the flock
For their spirits to slay

We call this darkness
We create our own hell
The terror is within us
The darkness is where we dwell

And the demons smile

God please forgive us
For our souls we may lose
The choices are ours
Yet the darkness we choose

God in Your Mercy
God in Your Peace
God in Your Love
Make this darkness decrease

Amen Amen Amen

Carry Us Through All Our Years

Out of the darkness
A voice cries out
Weak and muffled
It can not shout

Lord with all Your Mercy
Lord with all Your Might
Save this unholy sinner
From the darkest night

Burdened with our demons
Crippled by our fears
Tormented by our anguish
Drowning in our tears

Lord with all Your Mercy
Lord with all Your Might
Save this unholy sinner
From the darkest night

Choices most unholy
Deeds hidden in the night
Deals with those unworthy
Promised wealth and might

Lord with all Your Mercy
Lord with all Your Might
Save this unholy sinner
From the darkest night

Lord save us from our darkness
Cleanse us from our greed
Protect us from our demons
Stop our murderous needs

Lord with all Your Mercy
Lord with all Your Might
Save this unholy sinner
From the darkest night

Lord You are the Power
Lord You are the Way
Lord Your Holy Kingdom
Brings the Light of day

Bless us with Your Holiness
Wash away our fears
Consume us with the seeds of faith
Carry us through all our years

Amen Amen Amen

Screams In Silence

Lord too many of Your children are
without voices
For hell has taken its toll
The horror and the chaos
The cries of tortured souls

Those who scream in silence
Those who cry in the night
Have too long been from their Savior
In their choices between darkness and
Light

I ask that You would save us
I ask that You would send
Your Angels to walk among us
To bring this suffering to an end

Lord You can hear the screams in silence
Lord You can see the children die
Why do we waste away to ashes
When with You, our souls can fly

Lord protect us from our choices
Heal us from our sins
Guide us through this darkness
Let Your Angels in

That we may know Your Presence
That we may remember our Home
That we may awaken from the nightmares
And have our sins Atoned

Amen Amen Amen

Destruction

Lord, how long do we allow creation
to be tortured
For profit and for greed
The slaughter does not stop
For the killing, there is no need

The darkness in man
Forces species into extinction
Animals, plants and humans
Sometimes there is no distinction

What will be left
After mans destruction
Is there no hope
For the survival of creation

Who has the rights
Who has the need
For the salvation of creation
On my knees I do plead

Every life force of creation
Is a miracle unique
Save us from our darkness
We need Your Holy Voice to speak

God speak to the hearts
And souls of mankind
Heal their darkness
Heal their minds

Save us from ourselves
And the darkness we seek
Bless us with Your Mercy
We need Your Holy Voice to speak

Genocides and exterminations
Extinguish creation's life
God save the victims
Destruction is rife

God I do not understand
Man's need to destroy
These lives are precious
Not some unholy toys

God remind mankind
That they have Holy choices
Come into our lives
We need to hear Your Holy Voice

Amen Amen Amen

Coming Home

Lord Thank You

Lord thank You for my blessings
Engulf me and my family in the Holy
Light of the Lord
Help me to know and to do Your Will
to the best of my abilities

Consume me with Your Presence
Fill me with Your Grace
Let me hear Your Voice in these dark
places

Direct me in Your Ways
Carry me that I may conquer the
darkness
Protect me that I may not fear

Amen Amen Amen

Love Without Boundaries

Lord teach us to forgive others
As we ask You to forgive us

Lord teach us to love all Your creations
As we ask You to love us

Lord teach us to help and provide for
our brethren
As we ask You to help and provide
for us

Lord teach us to pray
That we may realize we can commune
with You directly

Without intermediaries
Without false gods
Without false prophets

God our Heavenly Father
Your Love for us has no boundaries
Teach us to Love as You do
Teach us to love unconditionally

Amen Amen Amen

Shatter The Death Masks

Lord help us to shatter the death
masks of this world
Lord help us to expose the darkness
within us to Your Holy Light

Lord hear our cries from the darkness
And make the path clear to us

Lord help us to Awaken
From the nightmares we have created

Lord help us to Awaken
From the illusions of this world

Lord help us to Awaken

Amen Amen Amen

Bless Me With Your Majesty

Ego is the darkness that holds us in this world

Ego is the darkness that makes us frail

Ego is the darkness that causes our fears and enrages our hatreds

Ego is not of God

Lord God please remove the barriers that separate me from You

Lord God please allow me to hear Your Voice

Lord God please conquer my ego

Lord God please bless me with Your Majesty

Amen Amen Amen

With My Voice

At Your feet I honor You my Lord
At Your feet I sing Your praise
At Your feet I cry tears of redemption
At Your feet

On my knees I will worship
My God
My Savior
My Redeemer
On my knees

With my voice
I will stand before You
I will sing Your Song
I will pray
With my voice

With my heart
I will surrender
I will surrender
I will surrender
With my heart

My Father

Amen Amen Amen

I Seek Your Face

Lord I want to cry out 'I seek
Your Face'
Yet, I know that as long as I am in this
world I will never be holy enough to
see the Face of God

Lord I want to cry out 'I seek
Your Face'
Yet, I know that as long as I am in this
world I will never be holy enough to
kneel at Your Feet

Lord I want to cry out 'I seek
Your Face'
That 'I long to hear Your Voice'
That 'I want to come Home'

Yet Lord, I believe I am in this world
for a purpose

Lord, I pray to You to use me
As a tool of Your Hand
As an instrument of Your Will

Use me Lord,
To bring Your Light to all the dark
places

Amen Amen Amen

The Holy Promise Of God

A promise so rich and pure
A promise like no other
A promise made by God the
Holy Father

A promise beyond our understanding
A promise beyond our world
A promise of Love eternal

A promise of Salvation
A promise of Redemption

God promised us a Savior
A King
A Lamb
A Prince

God sent us His Son
The Savior of all
The King of Heaven and earth
The Holiest of Lambs
The Prince of Peace

God let Thy Will be done

Amen Amen Amen

Lord I Come Before You

Lord I come before You this day
To ask for Your Love
To ask for Your Forgiveness
To ask for Your Mercy

Lord I come before You this day
To surrender my soul
To surrender my life
To surrender my heart

Lord I come before You this day
To ask You to direct me in all that I do
To ask You to use me to the best of my abilities
To ask You to give my life Holy purpose

Amen Amen Amen

Help Me Never To Forget

God gives me exactly what I need
When I need it

But sometimes when I receive these gifts
I do not recognize them immediately

They can come in many forms
In many ways

Sometimes it takes a long time for me
to realize the gift I have received

And sometimes I realize the miracle
immediately

Sometimes God heals me
By allowing me to heal others

Sometimes a walk through darkness
Brings me to a brilliant Light

Help me to never be so consumed
with darkness
That I can not be a tool of Your Will

Help me to never be so broken
That I can not pray

And help me never to forget

Amen Amen Amen

Open Our Hearts To Your Gifts

Lord open our hearts, our eyes and our beings
To Your Holy Majesty

Help us to realize that often the greatest gifts come in forms we do not expect
Help us to realize that You know what is best for us

Help us to remember that You Love us always
Help us to learn to recognize the gifts and miracles You send to us

God Bless us

Amen Amen Amen

Angels Protect

The Angels stood before me
As darkness sought to attack
Powerless against the Light
The monster behind the mask

The Angels hovered over
As I traveled these dark paths
To guide me and protect me
From the darkest wrath

My life here has a purpose
Though, yet I do not know
Why Angels hover over
And bless me where I go

I pray to God and Heaven
To use me during my stay
To help me be a voice
To bring light to show the Way

Amen Amen Amen

The Lights That Brighten This
World
Are Often Heaven Sent
To Guide Us Through Our
Darkness
As Only God Has Meant
Amen
Amen
Amen

www.ingramcontent.com/pod-product-compliance
Lightning Source LLC
Chambersburg PA
CBHW051709040426
42446CB00008B/799